THE DOG YEARS OF REEDUCATION

POEMS

THE DOG YEARS OF REEDUCATION

POEMS

JIANQING ZHENG

LAKE DALLAS, TEXAS

Requests for permission to reprint or reuse material
from this work should be sent to:

Permissions
Madville Publishing
PO Box 358
Lake Dallas, TX 75065

Cover Photo: Jianqing Zheng
Cover Design: Jacqueline Davis

ISBN: 978-1-956440-39-3 paperback
978-1-956440-40-9 ebook
Library of Congress Control Number: 2022944366

For Angela Ball, DC Berry, and Theodore Haddin

Contents

III

IV

In the Chinese Cultural Revolution (1966-1976), millions of middle school and high school graduates, called the *zhiqing* or *educated youth*, were sent to the mountains and countryside to receive reeducation from poor peasants. With a deep conviction that they would play some role in the transformation of rural China, the *zhiqing* became field hands, never realizing that reeducation was both a physical and psychological challenge. This collection of poetry relives those reeducation years in the fields. Half a century has passed, but memories remain as the historical presence of the hard times, each a page of suffering, cheering, or dreaming that turns for the reason of not forgetting.

I

rusticated years
lingering fog thinning
over frosted fields

Life in the Fields

Those years are like
a yellowed book
of memories with dog-ears
unable to smooth back.

Turning each page
is like unwrapping
an unearthed mummy,
dried but well preserved.

Picture-Taking in the Cultural Revolution

With a Chairman Mao badge
pinned on my cotton coat,

I pose for a graduation picture
while the short photographer

behind the camera ducks his head
under the black cloth to adjust the focus.

In a while he pops out and
asks me to look at his right hand

without blinking.
I stare and force a smile.

When the flashbulb glares, I blink.
In the resulting picture

only Mao's eyes are open.

Reel to Reel

1

Gene Kelly dances
under streetlight,
the taps snapping the wind

his black umbrella
pirouettes drops,
silver fireworks

the slanting rain
scissors his movements
into a shadow play.

An audience behind me
cracks melon seeds,
faint annoyance.

2

A young peasant
plows a rice paddy, shouting
"On, on" to the cow

his flax whip
splits the dry air
as if tearing a sheet

the burning sun
tans his body
into a pine stump.

My farm life
reels out of my mind,
the seed cracks reel in.

* *Singin' in the Rain* was shown in China in the late 1970s.

Star Watching

After graduating from a foreign language school in the Cultural Revolution, we have no choice but to go to the countryside to receive reeducation from the poor and lower-middle peasants. We learn to plow cotton fields, plant rice seedlings by hand, work barehanded, and walk barefoot.

> roosters crowing
> another day of life
> in the village

At night, our life is as flat as our farm work, tasteless as rice and pickled turnips we eat each day. No books to read, no chess to play, no dream to make. Luckily, Pigsy has a semiconductor radio. Lying in bed and smoking cheap cigarettes, we listen to the shortwave radio for comprehension of English. Sometimes we catch a couple of familiar words before we fall asleep.

> autumn night
> lying on rice stacks
> counting stars

Morning Chat

At fish-belly dawn, we
walk barefoot to the paddies.

Yi keeps yawning and complaining,
"Why get up so early to plant
rice seedlings? The sun is still in bed!"

Pigsy pats Yi on the shoulder,
"I heard you sip liquor till midnight."
"Really?" Yi quacks loudly.
"You must be my bedbug."

The sun is peeping
through a persimmon tree.

"Wow! What a big persimmon!"
Pigsy shouts loud. Pearl
jeers at him, "You like it? Go pick it.
It'll roast you into a Peking duck."

Horse sniffs, "That delicious?
I think he'll be a baked potato!"
Everyone clucks, "Yeah, a baked potato."

We roll up our pants and step
into the paddies to feed leeches.

Lunchtime

Back from the rice paddies for lunch, we slump down on the porch, listless as slugs. Chopsticks stir in bowls to pick out tiny rocks; white rice and brined turnips are as tasteless as day. A greenbottle fly humming like a drunkard wheels down on Pigsy's rice. Horse chuckles, eyes gloating, "Pigsy, you get a bowl of maggots. Do they taste good?" "Don't fart, buddy! You want to try some?" Pigsy shouts like vomit and casts rice over Horse. Everyone bursts out laughing: maggots wriggling on Horse's face.

plain laughter
flavor
of plain life

Break

The path between the paddies
    leads me to the lotus pond while
        the white sun squints through willows.

It's noon. Everything shuts its eyes.
    Only the cicadas' trill, louder
        and louder, floats over the pond.

I sit by a willow, light a cigarette.
    Smoke curls inside my throat,
        rushes out like light blue peonies.

A frog cools on the mossy stone.
    I move my foot toward it; it jumps in:
        circles of silver, circles of green.

I lie back yawning, eyes closed:
    thousands of stars are sparkling.
        The lotus scent nears.

The bell for work. I rub my eyes,
    light one more cigarette, and
        drag toward the field.

In the Cotton Fields

Cotton picking is as drab
as reciting Chairman Mao's
little red book.

Pigsy breaks into a song of
"Farewell to My Hometown."
We join him, and our husky voices
sandpaper the muggy heat. Girls
pick faster, their hands fluttering
like butterflies on cotton fluffs.

The noon sun is a bamboo steamer.
Sweat beads down my face,
I lick them in for my throat.

Pigsy edges up to Pearl,
"If I die of sunstroke, will you
wear a white flower and cry for me?"
Pearl's answer is as dry as a mummy,
"For you, I'll wear a cotton fluff."

My eyes blurring,
straw hats float like life preservers
in a white sea of cotton.

Lines for My Helpers

1
Spring wind:
    fecund smell
    of the tilled fields
    swings on the tail
    of the water buffalo

2
Summer evening:
    the cow chews cud
    by the shed
    as I go bathing
    in the creek

3
Autumn dusk:
    talk to the donkey
    hauling cotton
    on the rutty road
    to the village

4
Winter road:
    the horse and I
    deliver provisions
    to the peasants
    digging waterways

Road

When the bell tolls at sunset
I drag my feet out of the field
with a basket of cotton on my back.

Halfway to the village,
I kneel by a pond to scoop water
for my sweating face.

A red dragonfly
on a lotus bounces into the air
and glides away.

Then I sit against the basket,
eager for shuteye, but hunger
props me up and drags me

toward the village where
smoke threads over chimneys,
toward another night to dream home.

Before Supper

Pigsy sits dozing on the threshold,
chopsticks on a bowl by his side,

like a beggar. Pearl clucks to
chickens racing up for millet.

Wind stirs a green dragonfly
to rise like a helicopter,

sparrows tumble like falling leaves,
clouds dissolve their dark gray

to lacquer the sky into a cave.
In the distance, a military march:

hoofbeats, cannonades and drums
press in, louder:

a battle array of white rain
smashes the fermented air.

Pigsy opens sleepy eyes,
asking, "Mealtime?"

Back from the Cotton Trading Center

I holler at the donkey to trot faster because I want to get back to the village before nightfall, but it does not think my way. The sun retreats its light into embers surrounded by dark clouds; the dirt road is rutty; and the cart rocks me to shuteye. I dream of Mom cooking the pork rib soup I've been longing for. The snort shakes me up. Mouth watering, I jump off the cart, unharness the donkey, and lead it into the stable. On my way to my shanty, hunger growls like a cat. The moonrise looks like an empty yellow plate.

> autumn night
> serenaded
> by the cheerful katydids

Transplanting Seedlings

The sun rubs its eyes
and the green fields give off
a shimmering red.

We bundle rice seedlings
in the nursery bed
and carry them
in the bamboo baskets
to the paddies where
we toss the bundles. Then

we step into the muddy field
and move backward
with one hand grasping
a handful of seedlings
and the other planting
two or three of them.

We plant as fast as we can
to race with the rising sun
before it burns like a fireball
to blister our bent backs.

We remain silent as if
we must accept the fact that
our bodies deserve
bending or transplanting
like rice seedlings.

Rice Planting

Of all the farm jobs, planting rice with your bare hands and bent body under the hot sun is the least you tolerate, because leeches frequent your shanks to suck blood. When you feel the pain, the leeches already bloat with your blood. Filled with anger, you pull them off your shanks one by one, squeeze your blood out of their bodies, and fling them toward the dirt road. You look around with sweat streaming off your face like hot pee. Planters in the rice paddies look like exiles in the desert, and chinaberries along the creek look like Blackshirt soldiers. Cicadas shriek like the suppressed cry of the mind.

    sleepless night
    blistered back
    from sunburn

Burning

We reap rice as fast as we can
to escape sooner
from the burning sun.

Pigsy bundles behind and
shouts geeup at us
like we are donkeys.

Back from the threshing floor,
Wang mimics the chief,
"You must reap one more paddy."

Everyone straightens up,
staring with burning eyes
and yelling, "What?"

Horse throws Wang a look of pooh,
"Why not tell that fathead
we have been burned out?"

Thrusting his shoulder pole
into the field, Wang grumbles,
"I did, but he has no ears!"

Red-faced, Pigsy grunts,
"Folks, let's go for a break
in the shade. Geeup!"

We scuff to a willow
by the creek. In the paddy
Wang's shoulder pole

stands like an angry arm.

Cutting

When memory forms dull brown rust,
I take it off the hanger and whet it
into a shining sickle.
We walk in twos and threes
to the fields to cut wheat
waving and whispering in wind.

After reaping a large patch
we lie down, looking blankly
at the blue sky or cracking a joke.
Sometimes sparrows leap
and peck around as if interested
in what we laugh about.

The sun watches over us
like a coldhearted foreman.
His stare is a barking dog
to urge us to resume cutting
so the hot thug can bake our backs
into sizzling bacon.

Even a good girl twittering
like a wheatear would curse,
"This hot sun of bitch."
We swing our sickles until
the sun plops down with its blood
reddening the stubble fields.

Hunger

Go, slowly creaking oxcart—

Are you hungry? If you are,
stop and graze by the creek.
I'll try the sunset.
I don't even have ten *fens*
to buy a bowl of *re gan mian*
in a roadside eatery.
The setting sun on the horizon
is like a piece of ham
my stomach keeps rumbling for.

Go slowly, creaking oxcart—

Are you tired? If you are,
pull up on this dirt road
and have a break. I won't
shout, "On, on," at you.
I am tired of being tired,
of being told what to do.
I'm sure you are too.
Now on the horizon
half of the ham is finished.

Go, slowly creaking, oxcart—

Are you angry? If you are,
don't work tomorrow.
I hate to send food to villagers
digging the irrigation canal
twenty miles away. They never
ask me to stay for lunch
because each of them
has only one bowl of rice.
My stomach rumbles.

Go, slowly, creaking, oxcart—

I know you know the way
back to the village.
The sky is growing ash gray.
The sun has set within me.
I'm full, full of rumbles.

II

rice planting
I too
am a seedling

Night Life on the Farm

Night is fading in.
Young women wash clothes
by the creek.

Pigsy and Horse dive
off the stone bridge.
All they want is a moment
to be seen—a body exhibition.

On the porch, Yi pulls up
his pants to resume
his mosquito game.
The rest of us smoke
and listen to a serial
over a homemade radio.

Bang—we look up:
Yi holds up his hands,
chortles, "Come see
how many I've killed."

We run over to count
the mosquitoes
on his blood-stained palms
and shanks: only nine.

If he pats ten at a time
each of us will offer him
a cigarette, a precious award
since the cheapest pack
costs one whole day's farm work.

Killing for nothing,
Yi shakes his head
with a wry grin.
Suddenly he slaps
his face and shouts, "Ten!"

Night Swim

Perhaps tired of
sitting on the deck,
watching the new moon

drifting on the pale white
of the small pond and
hearing the frogs croaking

against the quiet night,
the man jumps up and
plops into the water

to startle the moon
into a flutter of wings,
but it rocks away

like an origami boat.
Then he flails the water,
intending to turn it over,

but it slithers away
like a silverfish. After
his moonplay,

the man rolls over
to backstroke and
float like a log

on the moonlit ripples
sparkling like fish scales.
He dog-paddles to shore

and sees the moon
shine like a paper lantern
above a weeping willow.

Night

After bathing in the pond,
I wrap myself in a towel
and trot back to my den.

Night ripples its gray
over the sky's last pink.

A flock of sparrows bursts
from the threshing floor.

Cordilleras of clouds rise
and fall in silhouette
like a trail of graves,
a pale moon for a wreath.

Somewhere in the village,
dogs are barking, possibly
chasing jackals.

Back in the room,
my roommate is asleep,
bubbling snores.

I light a cigarette
over the oil lamp.

In the next room,
a bedstead creaks
into deep night.

Playing Solitaire

On the roof
       a marching band of thunderstorm

Pigsy sweeps cards together
       to shuffle, one foot
              tapping impatiently

       a cigarette dangling
              at the corner of his mouth
                     its smoke threading
       vertically
& lengthening into a gray snake

       he casts cards forgetfully
           eyes half-closed
                & smoked to tears

       a spasm of cough—
           the ash
flakes down

When the storm slackens
       into rainwater
           dripping
              off the eaves
      & ticking
the puddle by the wall

            Pigsy leaps to his feet
         to push the window open—
       the smoke drifts out
            into evening haze

After Rain

Now on the wind,
thousands of gray horses
roll away the fevered air.

Green peppers, eggplants,
bok choy and pole beans
pallet the beds in sparkles.

Under a broken cart,
a few white ducks
preen their feathers.

Along the creek,
willows glaze with raindrops
like strings of crystals.

A croak stirs the quiet,
another one,
then a chorus of frogs.

I sit on the threshold
dabbing tobacco and dusk
into the cupped paper.

Indebted to Land

After dusk surges
across the sky,

> the moon appears
> over the village,

full and graceful
like a Tang Dynasty lady

> pacing in a red robe.
> In a while

it floats up
over the plowed fields,

> brightens
> like limelight,

and sways
its radiant sleeves

> as if ribbon-dancing
> with throws and spirals.

At this moment
you stand by the furrow

> and let petrichor
> enter your body

and soul—
a way to accept

> a way of life,
> a way to balance

the way of self
through hard times.

Lotus Picking

A small sampan slides through the dense green of lotus leaves, a girl sitting on the bow picks lotus seedpods by clipping their stems, and another girl stands in the stern, with her long black hair rippling in the breeze, rowing and singing, her lotus-picking song skimming and flapping like a great egret over the dark green lake and then soaring, hovering, flitting and swooping overhead. When the sampan glides to shore, the bird lands back on the shoulder of the rowing girl while lotus leaves whisper in the morning sunshine.

Man on the Front Porch

The setting sun recedes

    into

a red horse galloping in the distance

    into

the red lava flowing through the blue-black clouds

    into

the red eyes of a tired farmer leaning on the front porch

    into

a cigarette end making red dots at the corner of his mouth

    into

a starry night to release his body

    into

dreamland

Sick

Malaria befriends me. Chills and high fever pay their visits every hour. Cocooned in blankets, I shiver, teeth chattering. Cold sweat soaks my shirt. I unwrap myself, trying to clench my jaws. Dazed and dehydrated, I feel afloat like a life preserver. The red pills from the barefoot doctor don't work.

> summer night
> moonlight
> through the window
> a linen shroud
> wrapping me

Farmhands take me to the long-distance bus station, saying they want me to get treated in an urban hospital. I know I am always a stranger in their eyes. It's a stormy day. Thunder and lightning play symphonies. The bus jerks along slowly through the crisscrossing rain. I begin to feel better, knowing I won't die. I'm on my way home.

> Mom's tears
> flow into the soil
> of my heart
> the sickbed throbs
> with life

The Lesson Learned

When day and night
revolve like the duality
of yin and yang
way and no way
exertion and relaxation
positivity and negativity
earth and heaven
man and woman
city and countryside
dream and daydream,

we begin to see
reeducation as a coat
altered to wear,
a fate to face and
a life to live.

In our eyes,
the rugged path
winding to the fields
no longer looks sad
at sunrise, though
we don't know
when we can tread it flat
to prove the importance
of the lesson we've learned.

Sunset

Light recedes
field to field
into a big tomato
toothed in half by hills.

Hunger grows
chimney to chimney
and drifts like ribbonfish
among reefs of trees.

A cow mooing
slogs into a barn.

Bats take the sky,
dashing and flicking
in orange-red

which evaporates
to reappear
one window
at a time.

Catching

A girl who holds a net runs after a yellow butterfly all the way to the edge of the blooming canola fields shining in the warm spring sunlight. In a while, the butterfly flutters back. It dances in pitch and yaw over the girl's head. As she moves her net, the butterfly swoops and soars to evade her catch. Then it sheers back to the fields to bounce or alight from flower to flower. Pouting, the girl snaps a cluster of canola flowers and bounds back to the threshing floor where other girls play a hand-clapping game.

> dock fishing—
> waiting for a bite
> from the moon

One Winter Night

After wining and dining at a farmer's house,
I enter frozen midnight for my abode.
A touch of cold makes me tremble.

The moon peeps through broken clouds:
a marble tombstone in gray weeds.

I hiccup aloud Li Po's poetic lines:
"I look up at the bright moon and
lower my head to miss home."

That moonstruck poet. One night
drunken in a mooring boat, he wanted

to hug the river moon and drowned.
Along the wagon track covered with thin ice
weeping willows look like mourners.

I stagger on, whistling "Goodbye"
while the moonlight crunches under my feet.

Wintertime in the Village

Waking to a constant glint
on the window, I climb

out of bed to look outside—
the thick fallen snow sparkling

right before our dwelling.
On the other side of the creek

villagers' houses squat
like white sand dunes.

Willows along the creek
look cool in white dreads.

The creek has iced into
a smooth skating rink.

Awed by the snowscape,
I run out to wake up

my teammates. Everyone
comes out, half-awake

and shivering like birds
puffing up feathers, and then

scoot back to their nests.
Thanks to the heavy snow,

we rest for two good months
like pigs in the pen,

but the bone-chilling wind
slithers in at night

through the mud wall cracks
to turn our rooms

into iceboxes and us
into frozen fish.

Ode to Night

Coldness plasters
my hut
with thick snow

I quiver in bed
like a fish
caught and thrown

on the ice
to flop
in desperate throes.

III

homesick
a seesaw creaks
up and down

Question

Is this expansive flatland
where the flower drum song

roots deep and spreads wide,
where the sunset

promises a new dawn,
where cotton is handpicked

and rice is hand planted,
where rain is the source of life

also a dreamland studded
with starry wishes?

Memories

Ezra Pound, that great Imagist, said,
"Memories are the white hairs of the heart."

In the 1950s, in China, the whole nation
was galvanized to wipe out sparrows—

they ate grain. Then swarms of locusts
ate the whole country bare wherever they went.

When the Cultural Revolution spread like fire
the Red Guards from all over the country

crowded in Tiananmen Square to see
Chairman Mao, the reddest sun in their hearts,

rising on the tower. In tears, they shouted
a long, long life to him. On September 9, 1976,

the red sun sank for good. That afternoon,
we were picking cotton when a farmer

came over announcing, "Mao died."
His voice was a cool autumn breeze.

Maostalgia

I lost my voice in the Cultural Revolution after brandishing our great helmsman Mao's little red book and shouting my heart out for his longevity. Upon graduation from a boarding school of foreign languages, I answered Mao's call and went to the countryside to rebuild my body for strong bones and muscles. I even mastered the local dialect, excited that I could speak without an accent.

I heard of Mao's death while picking cotton. I was hungry that afternoon; I cursed the sun for not sinking faster; I cursed the bellman for not striking the bell sooner. A blur in my eyes and tremor, anxiety, and cold sweat all assailed me. At last, the sun set, bloody red, and the long tolling came from the village to drag me out of the fields.

> Great Wall tour—
> each souvenir stall sells
> Chairman Mao badges

Shouting

In October 1976, a month after
     Chairman Mao's death,

the village chief convened a meeting
     on the threshing floor.

He read a long editorial that
     endorsed the new leader, but

his reading sounded as flat
     as an unsalted dish.

Villagers began to chat about
     cotton price, nowhere

to buy chemical fertilizer,
     someone's son got married.

Realizing his reading was part
     of the noise buzzing

like a swarm of mosquitoes,
     the chief asked everyone

to be quiet. No one cared.
     Shaking his head, he thundered

"Long live Chairman Mao!"
     into the microphone. As if

awakened, we all stretched our arms
     to yawn the slogan after him.

Endurance

Your absence
like a heavy hammer
strikes my thought of you

into a dagger
shining cold and
hanging over my heart.

Each day
I forget you when I
bend my mind

in the paddy
to cut rice
with a sharp sickle,

but each night
when the moon peeks through
the broken window,

you appear
from nowhere
to slice my thought

into stripes
of pale moonlight
to bandage my wound.

The Gradation of Our Being

Day by day we wait to see
seeds sprout into a fuzzy green

and grow for a good harvest.
We have never felt

the land has grown us as well—
our hands calloused,

skin browned, minds furrowed,
and tongues localized.

We no longer look like a group
of urban youths

or sound like strangers
distanced by the peasants,

we have plowed our bodies
and sowed us as cottonseeds.

The Coming of Spring

You till the field all day to exude beads of sweat from your mind, but the downpour at night beats down rows, silts up furrows, and compacts soil as if to show you that tilling is no easy job. The field and the mind need a double plow to loosen and upturn to sprout into a fuzzy green.

weary night
stars breaking out
in a loud yawn

Waiting

This morning when I open
the envelope, your picture

slides out into my cold hand:
your eyes glisten

like sunshine on the iced
pond of my heart.

When will I go back to town?
I've been waiting the whole winter

in this dark room for a chink
of light while wind skids in

to shake me into a bare tree.
Teeth chattering, I clench

my desperation, listen to
frozen rain tinkling the leaking roof.

Letter to Girlfriend

You are a rice seedling I have grown in the paddy of my heart, a rope bridge I sway between city and country, a seesaw I use to keep ups and downs like the motion of sun and moon. Tell me when you want to smell the scent of new rice, and I will bring you a whole bag of it grown with my muddy hands. Let's promise to meet on that wooden bridge when we see each other again. Trust me, our yin-yang will spin forever like the earth under our feet.

caged days
a strong wish to hear
a magpie

Lamp

I stand on the wooden bridge
watching the glowworms
sparkling on and off over water
like a stream of stars,

while two barefoot boys
with jars in their hands
run to the riverside
to catch the blinks for fun.

Once in an evening
at boarding school,
I climbed over the wall
and ran to a nearby pond

to catch glowworms, wishing
they could be a flashlight
for me to read a ghost story
after lights out.

Pond Bathing

She steps out of her dress and
eases into the pond's gold.

Breast-deep in water,
she stretches her arms
to balance herself like a swan
about to flap into the sky.

Gilded winks ruffle around her;
she pushes them off in splashes.

The bun untied, and her dark hair
unfurls to meet the ripples.
She washes her hair
as if fingering harp strings.

Somewhere a flute
suddenly skims the pond.

Dream

I reap wheat
to wipe you off
like a drop of sweat,

but at night
you steal in and spade
my memory

into a song
of furrows soaked
in autumn rain,

fresh and earthy.

Notes

porch supper
offer a spoonful
to chickens

      spring breeze
      girls' giggling
      across the creek

dark night
chat about dream
by an oil lamp

      life in the fields
      a fly trapped
      in a web

dawnlight
in a rooster's crow
dimming stars

      tea-sipping
      reeducation years
      astringent again

the year of the pig
memory of farm life
oinks back

Dawn in the Village

The faded blue mist
moves over the plowed fields
like a monk in a long robe playing tai chi

the sparkling dewdrops
meditate in the lavender-blue flowers
of morning glories

the sun who had a night date
with Chang'e the moon goddess
rubs his eye and stretches his arms.

Soon his long dreads
wave among the slender branches
of weeping willows by the creek.

This is the moment
when the weary mind and body
drift in a light blue trance

while a dog at the edge of the village
barks like striking the bell
to urge us to go to the rice paddy.

IV

tallow stump
a new shoot shaking
in spring breeze

Goodbye

Excited as the mouse scooting
and squeaking on the roof beam,
I rise out of bed and fumble
for a match to light the oil lamp;
the room I've stayed in for three years
looks bleaker in a flash:
a desk and two beds are all
it will inherit. My roommate, Pigsy,
has gone to serve in the navy.

A rooster's crow somewhere.
I put the college admission letter
in my pocket and puff out the lamp,
ready to leave before daybreak
to avoid goodbye from workmates.
The door creaks open and closed
like a baby's mewling.
On the porch Hu stands alone
and hands me an umbrella,
the morning sky gray in drizzle.

Looking into Hu's eyes
black as bullet holes and desperate
as if with claustrophobia,
I crook a faint smile,
my mouth twitching without words.
Last night he cried over wine
at my farewell party. A handshake,
I throw myself into drizzle.

Before leaving the village,
I turn for the last look:
a string of my muddy footprints
running toward me.

Leaving the Village

Silence lies fallow everywhere
in the morning snow as if

to soothe the pain of my goodbye.
Like heart-warming charcoal fire,

you stand by the door seeing me off.
It's sad our geographies divide.

You root deep in the flatland
while I go away to find my dream.

Leaving you has been my desire
all these years. But,

I like you like I like a pretty girl,
because on my lips are

the scent of rice flowers and
sweetness of persimmons.

I bow to you for the folksongs
learned from you. I will miss you

when the katydids and stars
concoct memories.

Village in the Dream

The dirt road leads me through the mist to the village. By the creek, washing girls' laughter ripples over clothes batting, then a figure looms in with a wooden basket of clothes and bat—no longer the one reappearing before my eyes. I stroll on. A door creaks open, a middle-aged peasant with a hoe on his shoulder wobbles to the vegetable patch; he doesn't recognize me. We used to chat over liquor till daybreak. Four decades have long plowed away. Although my eager hand wants to lift the veil of memory, it has a heavy buildup of dust.

> a sip of oolong—
> rusticated years
> no longer taste bitter,
> in recollection
> a field of rice sprouts

Fireflies

After the sunset fades away,
fireflies start to blink
along the creek by the village,

their greenish light
on and off
like hide-and-seek.

Once waiting overnight
at the depot
for the morning train,

I climb to the top
of an abandoned carriage
to lie down and watch

the starry sky. When fireflies
glow around me,
I fling my hand to catch one,

wishing to see a blink
in my fist, but
I feel only an itchy crawl.

I open my hand and let it go.
High up in the sky, millions
of them are sparkling.

A Fleck of Warmth

The flutist, like a spirit,
is playing center stage. A tune

of remoteness brings back
my reeducation years—

the rugged dirt road
leading to the village

the irrigation canal
lined with weeping willows

the golden wheat
spreading faint scent at sunset

the wrinkle-faced blind man
who teaches me to sing folksongs

and the bamboo flute
I give to a schoolboy

when I leave for college.
Fifty years have eroded

the flow of consciousness
with no noticeable movement,

but there is always a chunk
of rock to strike a spark

in the mind, like this flute tune,
so close, so far away.

Jottings

Memories
    a burst of dry pods
        in the burning sun

        spring rain
    sesames inch by inch
up into flowering plants

summer dusk
    scent of rice
        brushed by breeze

        autumn haze
    loneliness drifts
over stubble fields

winter snow
    days of nothingness
        too white to stand

        night reading
    candlelight
a wavering prayer

cockcrow
    hope swells up from
        a pinpoint of daybreak

        dream gone
    snowdrift
rounds up the mind

Inlaid Images

When soybeans start to shoot flowers, I drive to the fields outside Itta Bena to see the tiny blossoms as if they are old friends I haven't met for a long time. Fifty years ago we were sent down to the countryside for reeducation. One day the local peasant took us to the soybean field to hoe weeds, and the purple flowers shy among green leaves caught our eye. Noticing our curiosity, he told us that tofu, soy sauce, soybean milk, and vegetable oil were all made from soybeans. To add a taste to our learning lesson, he asked his wife to cook for us a big bowl of homemade tofu as tender as the soybean flower and as beautiful as their hearts.

> lily of the valley
> brushed by spring breeze
> the village girl's smile

Looking Back

If I
never tilled rice paddies at sunrise
never handpicked cotton under blue skies
never dug irrigation canals in winters
never mucked out stables before dusk
never smelled purple soybean flowers

if leeches
never sucked blood from my shanks, calluses
never formed hard and thick on my palms, the sun
never blistered my back

if I
never acquainted myself with local peasants
never worked with them shoulder to shoulder
never chatted with them in their shacks
never witnessed the joy and pain of their life

if all this
never was a part of reeducation, I could
never relate grains to drops of sweat and
never imagine the oil lamp as the light of hope.

Five decades have long gone.
My body has become a rusty plow.
Some nights I dream of tilling at sunrise or
reading in the deep night with a desire
to turn to a new page of life.

Stranger

Fifty years ago I was dispatched to a remote village for reeducation. After jumping off a truck at a distribution center, I carried my belongings on my back and followed a dirt track winding mile after mile to my destination. When I got there, the sunset was the first to welcome me with a warm hug. That night wrapped in bed like a netted fish, I felt that footslogging to the village was my first lesson to learn though I wondered why I must be sent to a strange place.

loud rooster
waking
to a slither of light

Old Days in the Fields

are cotton crop residues
used as organic fertilizers
to enrich the soil of mind
with its long roots woven
into a chic braid trimmed
on the back of the head

are dried dates preserved
to chew slowly because
they are the fruits that
have absorbed sunshine
and moonlight, feeling
and sweat, dew and rain

are memories tempered
hard and sharp with pains

A Momentary Stay

As you carefully unstuck
the diary pages yellowed
with cigarette burns
and tea stains, words
come alive into a group of
young people hoeing weeds,
planting rice at dawn,
picking cotton till the bell
strikes the sun down,
lying frazzled on straw stacks,
stargazing without being able
to see a dim glow of future,
and getting drunk in order
to throw up our hardships.

One hot summer night
after each drank a bowl
of kaoliang liquor,
we jump in the creek
to sober up fast, but
the desire to feel sober
is not being sober.
Life is still as lifeless
as a gray clay vessel
in a still life painting.

Turning page after page,
memories are stirred up
like dust spiraling
in the shaft of sunlight
cast onto the mindscape
where old days lie at rest
in dead silence.

A Dog-eared Page

One day a new acquaintance came over to chat over coffee in my apartment when I served as a Fulbright Scholar at his university. He bragged about his book collection—ten thousand shelved books almost touched the ceiling of his study.

> harvest break
> wind and sunshine chasing
> over wheat

Like a glib-tongued salesman, he persuaded me to buy a volume of Chinese history and culture for self-study. I wowed at his bookucation, uttered, "You must be a fat bookworm. Have you bitten all your books?" He shook his head shyly. A librarian for thirty years, he had an irresistible desire for books.

> waiting for lunch
> an ant crawling
> in my empty bowl

One evening after taking my after-dinner walk, I went to his condo to borrow a book about reeducation in the Cultural Revolution. Sitting in his tiny study where a leg stretch would knock down a pagoda of books, I opened the one I wanted: two fat bookworms cruising on a dog-eared page.

> bell striking
> the moon over fields
> folded in half

The Persistence of Memory

The mud-wall dwelling has been plastered
    in my brittle memory for fifty years.

The three rooms on the west end belonged
    to seven girls. They chatted like birds

in the evening tree. What are they now?
    Mothers, grannies, wives, or damas

dancing in the square, dozing
    before TV or babysitting grandkids?

On the east end was the kitchen where
    Pigsy cooked us three meals per day.

Next to it was the storage for rice and
    cotton stalks used to stoke the cooking fire.

Other rooms were for the boys. The first
    was Drum's. The two knives kept

under his pillow scared Tiger away, so
    Pigsy and I adopted the roomless cat.

The next was Hu and Farting Wheel's,
    then Kim and Wang's, Xiaoyi and Horse's.

The fifth was ours. The moldy smell
    hangs like a spiderweb. There used to be

three plain beds with straw mattresses,
    three wobbly stools, one desk,

one kerosene lamp, and one basin stand.
    When the roof leaked, we put washbasins

on the mosquito nets, but the rainwater
　　leaked in to stain our nets into a world map.

After picking cotton the whole day,
　　we sat on the porch like drooping sunflowers,

whining "Goodbye to the River City"
　　in a long drawl. We also stayed up late,

smoking Big Rooster and gazing at
　　the stars for a bright tomorrow

though we never knew when we would
　　swim back to our river city.

Acknowledgments

Warmest thanks to Angela Ball, DC Berry, Kimberly Davis, Ted Haddin, Linda Parsons, and Madville Publishing for providing gracious support and invaluable comments on this poetry collection. Grateful acknowledgment is made to the following journals, where these poems, or earlier versions of them, originally appeared:

A Hundred Gourds: "Catching"
Blue Mountain Review: "Question," "Life in the Fields" (formerly titled "Rusticated Life")
Broad River Review: "A Fleck of Warmth"
Connecticut River Review: "Before Supper," "Break," "Road," "Goodbye"
Contemporary Haibun: "Lotus Picking," "Maostalgia," "Rice Planting," "Sick," "Star Watching," "Village in the Dream"
Enforced Rustication in the Chinese Cultural Revolution: "Notes"
English Journal: "Lamp," "Man on the Front Porch"
Fireflies' Light: "Jottings," "Old Days in the Fields," "Rusticated Years"
Hanging Loose: "Hunger," "Picture-Taking in the Cultural Revolution"
Jabberwock Review: "Night Swim"
Mankato Poetry Review: "After Rain"
Mississippi Review: "Sunset"
New World Writing Quarterly: "A Dog-eared Page," "Back from the Cotton Trading Center," "Endurance," "Leaving the Village," "Lines for My Helpers," "Ode to Night," "Stranger," "The Gradation of Our Being"
North of Oxford: "Indebted to Land," "Looking Back"
Plainsongs: "In the Cotton Fields," "Night Life on the Farm"
Poetic Eloquence: "Pond Bathing"
Poetry Midwest: "Playing Solitaire"
POMPA: "Fireflies," "Memories"
Presence: "Inlaid Images"
Rattle: "Night"
Red River Review: "Lunchtime," "Shouting"
Southern Poetry Review: "Reel to Reel"
Storyboard: "Burning," "Waiting"
The Kerf: "One Winter Night"
The Plaza (Japan): "Morning Chat"
Under the Basho: "Letter to Girlfriend"

About the Author

Jianqing Zheng is the author of *A Way of Looking* and two poetry chapbooks, editor of *Conversations with Dana Gioia, Sonia Sanchez's Poetic Spirit through Haiku*, and five other books. He received the 2019 Gerald Cable Book Prize and two literary arts fellowships from the Mississippi Arts Commission, among other awards and honors. He is professor of English at Mississippi Valley State University, where he serves as editor of the *Journal of Ethnic American Literature* and *Valley Voices* and is the former editor of *Poetry South*. A reeducated youth in the Chinese Cultural Revolution, Zheng has lived in Mississippi since 1991.

Lightning Source UK Ltd.
Milton Keynes UK
UKHW012029130223
416963UK00009B/109